Bárbara Pötter Pereira

Regional Development and the High-Tech Industry

Bárbara Pötter Pereira

Regional Development and the High-Tech Industry

The prospects and needs of the high-tech industry as seen by the regional market of Santa Maria - RS

ScienciaScripts

Imprint

Cover image: www.ingimage.com

This book is a translation from the original published under ISBN 978-3-330-77151-2.

Publisher:
Sciencia Scripts
is a trademark of
Dodo Books Indian Ocean Ltd. and OmniScriptum S.R.L publishing group

120 High Road, East Finchley, London, N2 9ED, United Kingdom
Str. Armeneasca 28/1, office 1, Chisinau MD-2012, Republic of Moldova, Europe
Managing Directors: Ieva Konstantinova, Victoria Ursu
info@omniscriptum.com

Printed at: see last page
ISBN: 978-620-8-63821-4

SUMMARY

SUMMARY

REGIONAL DEVELOPMENT AND INDUSTRY FROM HIGH TECHNOLOGY

In several countries, the creation of technology parks has been on the rise, with the aim of creating the right conditions for the development of innovations, which are so necessary for the sustainability and competitiveness of companies and nations. In Santa Maria, RS, a new technology park is being built by the Federal University of Santa Maria, in partnership with the city council and the World Bank, as well as important local institutions. It is therefore necessary for society to turn its attention to the success of this venture, making efforts to contribute to its success. In view of this, the problem of this research is to investigate how the dynamics of the local and regional market in Santa Maria can influence the performance of technology-based companies set up in this enterprise. Using bibliographical research and empirical data collection through questionnaires, it was possible to observe that the sustainability and competitiveness of technology-based enterprises can be influenced by opportunities for product experimentation, evaluations and *feedback* from the local and regional market, and that the region's industries are open to offering innovative solutions for their businesses.

Key words: Regional market. Technology-based entrepreneurship. Technology parks.

1 INTRODUCTION

The creation of technology-based companies makes it possible to create highly qualified jobs, generates foreign currency for society and promotes the creation of greater innovative dynamics for national industry. These companies are therefore of great importance to society (MINARDI *et al.,* 2013).

Micro or small technology-based companies are industrial organizations with fewer than one hundred employees, or companies that provide services and have fewer than fifty employees, which are committed to the design, development and production of new products or processes, and are characterized by the systematic application of technical and scientific knowledge (ARAGÂO, 2005).

In various countries, there have been growing initiatives to reproduce the ideal environments for the development of technology-based companies, such as Silicon Valley in the United States (BARQUETTE, 2002, PALETTA, 2008). A fact that has been widely observed is the existence of a relationship between the emergence of high-tech companies and the physical proximity of large university institutions and/or technological research institutions (BIZZOTTO *et al.*, 2002; SANTOS, 2004; ANDRADE JUNIOR, 2012).

The creation of Technology Parks in developed countries has been an inspiration to the whole world (GARGIONE, 2011). These ventures function as important policy instruments to support innovation, make it possible to transfer technology, generate new jobs and favor economic and social development (MACHADO *et al.,* 2005; GARGIONE *et al.,* 2006).

Considering that the Santa Maria Technology Park is under construction, set up by the Federal University of Santa Maria, in partnership with city hall, the state government, industrial associations and social and business entities and the World Bank, it is important that society turns its attention to the performance and success of this enterprise, making efforts to contribute to its success.

Given these propositions, this investigation seeks to address the following research problem: how can the dynamics of the local and regional market in Santa Maria influence the performance of technology-based companies set up in the Santa Maria Technology Park?

Considering the above problem, this study deals with the interrelationship between the local and regional market of Santa Maria and the performance of technology-based companies to be installed in the Santa Maria Industrial Park. Its aim is to investigate the possible mutually beneficial relationships between the industries of Corede Central and the technology-based companies set up in the Santa Maria Technology Park.

In order to do this, the Corede Central Region of Rio Grande do Sul will be investigating aspects that can influence the sustainability and competitiveness of technology-based ventures; the profile of the regional innovation needs of the industries in the Corede Central region will be surveyed; and the aspects that hinder innovation, in the perception of the Corede Central industries, will be investigated.

It is important to bear in mind that decisions related to entrepreneurship are associated with the perception and comparison of opportunities, which when observed and managed can favor greater and more sustainable local or regional economic development (SCHUMPETER, 1984; CASTANHAR, 2007; STEPHENS and PARTRIDGE, 8

2011). In this sense, this work is important as it provides data on local industries, which can guide and support strategic decisions by technology-based companies that are part of, or intend to join, the Santa Maria Technology Park.

This research is characterized by its exploratory nature, defined by Gil (2006) as being the nature of investigations that seek to provide familiarity with a problem in order to make it explicit. It is also descriptive, in that it describes phenomena or populations, and/or the relationships between their variables

(MALHOTRA, 2006).

Two data collection methods were used. Initially, data was obtained from the literature on the subject, which made it possible for the author to orient herself in relation to the theoretical underpinnings of the subject. According to Silva and Meneses (2005), bibliographical research is research based on already published material, consisting mainly of books, journal articles and material available on the internet.

In its empirical data collection phase, a structured questionnaire was used with 14 industries in the Corede Central region that employ more than 100 people. These industries represent 50% of the total universe. A structured questionnaire is one in which individuals choose the answer that best represents their opinion through closed questions (GIL, 1999). The data was treated using a quantitative approach, defined as "that which translates opinions and information into numbers in order to classify and analyze them" (SILVA; MENESES, 2005, p.20).

The aim of this study is to identify the possible synergistic relationships between the industries of Corede Central and the technology-based companies located in the Santa Maria Technology Park. In other words, how the local and regional markets can influence technology-based ventures, and what is the profile of the needs of market agents that can constitute opportunities for companies operating in this technology park.

In the interest of achieving a good organization of the research work, the work was divided into two stages, each embodied in an article. The first seeks to demonstrate how the local and regional markets can influence the ability of technology-based ventures to sustain themselves and be competitive; and the second seeks to identify the profile of regional innovation needs, which may constitute opportunities for technology-based companies installed in the Santa Maria Technology Park.

2 ARTICLE 1 - THE IMPORTANCE OF THE LOCAL/REGIONAL MARKET IN THE SUSTAINABILITY OF NEW TECHNOLOGY-BASED VENTURES: A STUDY FROM PORTER'S PERSPECTIVE

Bàrbara Potter Pereira[1] Janis Elisa Ruppenthal[2]

SUMMARY

Technology-based companies are characterized by developing products, processes or services resulting from applied research, and have innovation as their main focus. Entrepreneurship in this type of business is a highly complex task which is of great importance as a factor in regional development, by stimulating the economic system, job creation and the competitiveness of companies in the region. The latter, in turn, when demanding, allow the technology-based company to observe and satisfy emerging needs, which becomes an incentive for innovation. Based on the relevant literature, this study analyzes how the local and regional market can influence the sustainability and competitiveness of these ventures, by investigating which premises, when met, can be beneficial to their development. It was observed that the main environmental factors exerting such influences are: the existence of highly qualified staff; the establishment of close relations with local companies, providing opportunities for product experimentation, evaluations and *feedback*; and interaction with a demanding consumer public, so as to exert pressure for continuous improvement in the quality of their products, and to stimulate the creation of innovations.

Key words: Entrepreneurship. Technology-based companies. Environmental factors.

INTRODUCTION

Entrepreneurship is a phenomenon permeated with complexity, characterized

1 Administrator, Master in Production Engineering from USFM.
2 PhD in Engineering. Professor in the Postgraduate Program at UFSM.

by people developing their businesses in such a way as to involve any form of innovation related to the prosperity of organizations (DOLABELA, 1999).

It is a social phenomenon (DOLABELA, 2006; SHANE, 2012) that is oriented towards taking advantage of business opportunities, through new ways of using resources and innovation, in order to promote the dynamics of economic cycles. In particular, for this author, entrepreneurship and innovation are related categories, and the categories that relate entrepreneurship to technological innovations are: the manufacture of new goods; new production methods; the opening up of new markets; the acquisition of new sources of raw materials; and the creation of a new economic organization (SCHUMPETER, 1982).

However, entrepreneurship is a highly complex task, as evidenced by the fact that for every 100 micro and small enterprises (MSEs) opened in Brazil, around 27 do not remain in operation until they have been in business for two years (BRASIL, 2013). Entrepreneurship is of great importance as a factor in regional economic development, highlighting the importance of entrepreneurial individuals, who take risks when undertaking, as stimulators of the economic system, detectors of opportunities, creators of jobs and drivers of development (SCHUMPETER, 1982).

Its occurrence, however, is linked to different factors. In developing countries, entrepreneurial actions out of necessity are common, in the face of unemployment and few local job opportunities. In more economically developed nations, opportunistic entrepreneurial strategies, in which individuals perceive an opportunity and create ways to take advantage of it, are more common and advantageous, both for them and for society (CHIAVENATO, 2008; GRECO *et al.*, 2010).

The decision to undertake or not results, among other things, from comparing the opportunities available, which allow people or organizations to exploit identified potentials and obtain a certain return (CASTANHAR, 2007). These potentials are constituent elements of what is generally known as the market, and they stand out the larger the network of inter-organizational relationships between companies. The network of relationships is capable of broadening communication, obtaining new customers, suppliers, technological partners and funding bodies, as well as interpersonal relationships that can bring benefits of different kinds (GALLON *et al., 2009;* BARBOSA *et al.*, 2012).

In this sense, entrepreneurs in a given market are dependent on the relationships they establish in their local bases, taking into account what Porter (1999a) advocates, for whom the decisive characteristics of a place enable its companies to create and sustain competitive advantages in specific fields, as long as there is a healthy interrelationship between companies, government bodies, universities, among other social and economic actors.

In the case of technology-based companies (TBEs), which are characterized by developing products, processes or services resulting from applied research (BRASIL, 2000), the organizations that make up the local market where they operate, when demanding, are important because they allow them to glimpse and satisfy emerging needs, which becomes incentives for innovation (PORTER, 1999a). In view of these premises, this work seeks to investigate the following problem: How can local and regional markets influence the ability of technology-based ventures to sustain themselves and remain competitive? In view of this question, the aim of this work is to investigate which premises, when met, can be beneficial to the development of high-tech manufacturing companies.

The technique used to carry out this research is that of bibliographical investigation, looking at the different studies and approaches available in the literature to find the theoretical contributions that will lead to clarification of the issue under study. The work is structured in four sections, the first of which is this introduction. The second section presents the concepts and assumptions about the importance of innovation as a strategy for sustainability and competition between companies. Next, the main aspects related to high-tech business ventures are described and then, in the light of Porter's theory of the competitiveness of nations, the importance of a demanding local market for the success of local ventures is described. Finally, the conclusions of this reflection are presented.

TECHNOLOGY-BASED VENTURES

According to the Organization for Economic Cooperation and Development in Europe - OECD (2004), the creation and diffusion of new technologies are essential for production growth and increased productivity. Within industry, innovation can be categorized in different ways: a) the introduction of a new product or a change in the quality of an existing product; b) innovation in the production process, which constitutes a real novelty for the industry; c) the opening up of a new market; d) the generation of new sources of supply of raw materials or other inputs; e) changes in industrial organization, such as the implementation of new product marketing methods.

A technology-based company is one that uses the systematic application of scientific and technological knowledge in various areas, used alone or in combination, to develop technological innovation or new products, processes and services. For example, a company that develops *software,* i.e. develops technology, is considered to be technology-based (UNIVERSIDADE FEDERAL DE LAVRAS, 2011).

According to Perussi Filho (2006), technology-based companies are organizations whose activity requires the generation or intensive use of technologies to generate innovation in the form of new products, processes and services. They develop and deploy more complex technologies, designed to collaborate with their customers and partners, equipping them with the tools, information and support they need to use increasingly sophisticated and efficient solutions to achieve their business objectives and goals (REF and LEE, 2009).

Most technology-based companies originate in *spin-offs* from projects developed by universities and research centers, which have specialized human resources and invest in infrastructure for research and knowledge creation. The main objective of these companies is technological development based on their ability to identify and develop new technologies with a high potential to generate profit in the market, and also on their capacity for rapid growth, based on the successful introduction of technologies (FONSECA *et al.*, 2012).

For Barquette (2002, p.102), the typical dynamics of the establishment of EBTs include, among other factors, the existence of certain local conditions, or *location factors*, which contribute to the formation of an environment favorable to the emergence and sustainability of creative potential. The local confluence of elements favorable to the development of these companies is called the *innovative environment.* Without these factors, the effectiveness of establishing this type of industry will be limited to the limits imposed by the economic cycles typical of this sector. In short, it can be said that "a truly innovative society cannot be built in a place without certain locational elements".

According to Barquette (2002), the elements that favor the establishment of high-tech industries are described in table 2 below:

Table 1 - locational factors that make up the innovative environment

Workforce (qualitative aspects)	Quality of life
Capital	Possibility of vertical integration
Local science base	Conditions of access to information
Neighborhood to metropolises and research-oriented universities	Business profile of the local community
Telecommunications and Transportation	Working with partners in the public sector, trade associations, institutions, individuals, etc.

Source: Barquette (2002).

Therefore, the favorable environment referred to by Barquette (2002) indicates some criteria which, when met, enable high-tech companies to succeed in the market. These include the profile of existing companies in the community, which can influence the performance and opportunities for EBTs to create innovations.

Bercovich and Swanke (2003) cited interactions with local customers as opportunities from a technological point of view; even if commercially they don't represent significant profitability, if there is proximity and trust there can be opportunities for experimentation and *feedback*, which are important for companies developing technology and innovations.

For Porter (1999a), in order to achieve competitive success, organizations need to know the five essential forces in the structural analysis of industries. In doing so, they will be able to adopt appropriate strategies for the different situations in which they find themselves. These are: new entrants, buyers, substitute products, suppliers and competitors.

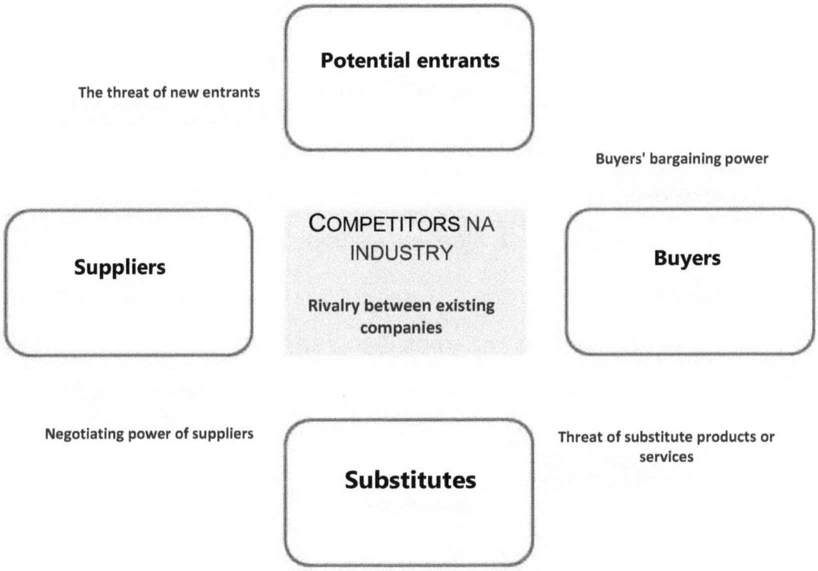

Figure 1 - Porter's five forces Source: Adapted from Porter (1999a).

Another important consideration is that it is now possible for medium-sized and small companies to have access to benefits that previously only large companies had and, as a result, to become more agile by adding advantages in technology or logistics (CASAROTTO FILHO, 2001).

INNOVATION AS A CONDITION FOR SUSTAINABILITY

The socio-economic, political, environmental and cultural transformations the world has experienced, especially in the last decades of the 20th century, have led to significant changes in the business landscape and have stimulated the need for new discussions and solutions the competitiveness of companies in the market. Increasingly complex activities carried out by companies now require them to operate, not infrequently, in association or partnership with other companies, in order to increase productivity, rationalize costs, reduce environmental impacts, promote economic efficiency and, ultimately, their own sustainability (CASAROTTO FILHO, 2001; BARROS *et al.*, 2010).

The concept of corporate sustainability is associated with the practice of "ensuring the long-term success of the business, while at the same time contributing to the economic and social development of the community, a healthy environment and a stable society". In this way, sustainable companies are not just those that make a profit, but those that, in carrying out their activities, provide some kind of profit for society, even if this profit does not only translate into financial gains, but also into social and environmental gains (ETHOS, 2013).

In addition, the sustainability of companies is increasingly linked to innovation. This model functions as a response to institutional pressures, through which the market demands organizations capable of innovating efficiently in economic terms, without losing sight of social and environmental responsibility. Organizations of this type aim for competitive advantages by developing new or modified products, services, processes and businesses, in order to meet the specific needs imposed by society, and having this profile has become a competitive factor, whether in terms of differentiation or the necessary qualification to continue in the market (PORTER, 1999a; BARBIERI *et al.*, 2010).

Innovation is a set of improvements, both technological and methodological, aimed at adapting the company and its products and/or services to market demands. Factors that can put pressure on the creation of innovations are new technologies launched by competitors, new or renewed buyer needs, fluctuations in input costs, or changes in government regulations. These are important aspects which, when perceived early, can result in competitive advantages for those who somehow exploit them (WONG and SINGH, 2004; PORTER and KRAMER, 2009).

Van der Meer (2007) states that innovation is strongly associated with entrepreneurship, and its use is generally related to the creation or increase of competitive advantages for organizations, and the greater the quantity and quality of innovations they promote, the more successful they tend to be in the pursuit of their objectives. Companies can develop anything from simple cost-benefit ratios for their products to a competitive standard capable of changing the model in force before the innovation (TIDD, 2001).

With innovations that increase productivity, companies gain cost advantages over their competitors, allowing them to operate with a higher profit margin or even to charge lower prices than the competition in order to gain a greater share of the market. In cases where the product is an innovation, companies obtain a legal monopoly or a patent, which guarantees them greater profitability (OECD, 2004).

It is also important to note that innovative behavior does not have to be limited to the daily life of larger companies. Small companies can and should also innovate, and the adoption of a pattern of innovative behavior is more related to the vision of entrepreneurs than to issues such as access to financial resources (MARKOVITC, 2006; PEREIRA *et al.*, 2009).

IMPORTANCE OF THE DEMANDING LOCAL MARKET

Porter (1999b, p.210) points out that companies have a strong interest in the business environment their locality, and this interest exceeds the importance of taxes, electricity costs and wage levels. Important competitive advantages of a lasting nature are related to local factors, which include situations such as the grouping or clustering of rival companies and industries, which end up establishing favorable conditions for the development of local economic growth strategies.

Porter (1999b) points out that the competitiveness of local industries is related to the capacity for innovation that these industries acquire, as they receive pressure from the companies that compete with them, at the same time as they are pressured by their buyers. Because they are subjected to constant challenges, these industries end up benefiting from being able to adapt to continuous improvement and from developing the conditions to react quickly to market demands and inclement weather. The variables that benefit these industries include strong competitors, aggressive suppliers and demanding consumers in their own market, which makes them innovate more quickly and efficiently, obtaining important competitive advantages (PORTER, 1999b).

Demanding customers, according to Porter (1999b), are capable of stimulating the development of innovations that improve the quality of products, reducing production costs and, consequently, enabling the business to compete better.

Today, at a time when the focus of companies and businesses is on quality and customer satisfaction, customer needs and constant technological changes are of great importance in determining the competitiveness of locations (MORAES and MARTINS, 2006; EDLER and GEORGHIOU, 2007).

Porter (1999b) states that the local market has the advantage of the spatial proximity of related and supporting sectors upstream and downstream, making it easier to exchange information and stimulating a successive exchange of ideas and innovation. In addition, companies that produce with sufficient quality to meet the demands of their local consumers should, in advance, reach a level of quality suitable for competition in foreign markets and for export, which should ensure greater profitability through gains in scale (PORTER, 1998; JOÂO, 2008).

On the other hand, Barquette (2002) states that the proximity and size of consumer markets are not preponderant variables for the success of EBTs, but the existence of a local market with easier access should not be ignored in its importance.

From an economic point of view, innovation can contribute to the effective commercial exploitation of new ideas, promoting sustainable growth and prosperity. However, not everything that is considered innovative for one region is innovative for another. In view of this, it is important to establish relationships and interactions with different sectors and segments of the local economy, such as agriculture, information and communication technology, transport and energy companies, among others, in order to meet territorial needs (DEMARTY, 2006).

According to Barquette (2002), because the new industries are based heavily on science and rely heavily on innovation, one of the key elements in choosing their location has become the presence of highly qualified professionals, both entrepreneurs and employees, who bring together knowledge in specific areas across a broad spectrum, such as IT. In this way, not only can technology-based industries contribute to the development of the region where they operate, but they also need to have some degree of development where they are located, to the point where they can be provided with some essential resources, such as people who are suitable for the job.

FINAL CONSIDERATIONS

Enterprises based on high-tech production are of great importance to the productive world, since they promote the innovation that is so necessary for the competitiveness of business organizations, especially industry, ultimately benefiting society as a whole. In addition to the cost advantages over competitors, innovations also have the characteristic of being able to benefit companies of different sizes, leading them to a greater ability to compete, including in markets outside their regions.

Technology-based companies can operate by introducing new products or improving the quality of existing products; innovating production processes; opening up new markets and creating alternatives for the supply of raw materials. However, their success depends on the existence of elements favorable to their development in their operating environment. It is therefore a question of how the local market influences their ability to sustain themselves and be competitive.

Among these factors are: the existence of highly qualified personnel; the establishment of close relations with local companies, in order to supply their demands and those of their clients, providing, if not significant income, at least opportunities for product experimentation, evaluations and *feedback*, which are important for improving the quality of production.

In addition, in line with Porter's recommendations, it is important that these types of companies interact with a demanding consumer public in their local market, so as to exert pressure for continuous improvement in the quality of their products and stimulate the creation of innovations.

REFERENCES

BALLANTINE, B.; DEVONALD, B.; MEADS, R. The power of customers to drive innovation. A report by business decisions limited for the enterprise directorate general of the European Commission. Brussels, 2003.

BARBOSA, D.M.S.; NORONHA, N.S.; CASTRO, C.C. Entrepreneurship, innovation and relationship networks: the case of an incubated company. Espacios, v.33, n.11, p. 10-16, 2012.

BARBIERI, J.C.; VASCONCELOS, I.F.G.; ANDREASSI, T.; VASCONCELOS,

F.C. Innovation and sustainability: new models and proposals. Revista de Administraçâo -RAE, v. 50 - n. 2 - apr./jun. 2010 - 146-154

BARROS, R.A.; ANDRADE, E.LO.; VASCONCELOS, A.C.F. Practices of corporate sustainability in the footwear APL of Campina Grande - PB: a case study. Revista Gestâo Industrial, v. 6, n. 01: p. 157-177, 2010.

BERCOVICH, N.; SWANKE, C. Cooperation and competitiveness in the software industry of Blumenau. Santiago de Chile: Cepal, 2003.

BRAZIL. Survival and mortality. 2013. [on line]. Available at: <http://www.brasil.gov.br/empreendedor/empreendedorismo-hoje/sobrevivencia-e-mortalidade>. Accessed on: May 20, 2013.

BRAZIL. Manual for the implementation of business incubators: technical report. Brasilia: Ministry of Science and Technology, 2000.

CASAROTTO FILHO, N.; PIRES, L.H. Redes de pequenas e médias empresas e desenvolvimento local. Sâo Paulo: Atlas, 2001.

CHIAVENATO, I. Empreendedorismo: dando asas ao espirito empreendedor. 3ª. ed. Sâo Paulo: Saraiva, 2008.

DEMARTY, J.L. Innovation in Leader+. European Commission Leader+ Magazine, V.5, p.3, 2006.

DOLABELA, F. Oficina do Empreendedor. Sâo Paulo: Cultura Editores Associados, 1999.

DOLABELA, F. Luisa's secret. 30. ed. Sâo. Paulo: Editora de Cultura, 2006.

EDLER, J; GEORGHIOU, L. Public procurement and innovation - Resurrecting the demand side. Research Policy, v.36, p. 949-963, 2007.

FONSECA, R.G.C.; CLEMENTE, R.G.; OLIVEIRA, A.R. evaluation of knowledge management practices adopted in new technology-based ventures. Revista de Gestâo e Operçôes Produtivas, v.3, p.2-12, 2012.

GALLON, A. V.; ENSSLIN, S. R.; SILVEIRA, A. Relationship network in incubated technology-based companies (EBTS): a study of its importance for organizational performance in the perception of entrepreneurs. Revista de Gestâo da Tecnologia e de Sistemas de Informaçâo, v.6, n.3, p. 551-572, 2009.

GRECO, S.M.S.; FRIEDLANDER JR., R.H.; DUARTE, E.C.V.; RISSETE, C.R.; FELIX, J.C.; MACEDO, M.M.; PALADINO, G. Entrepreneurship in Brazil. 2010. Curitiba: IBQP, 2010.

JOÂO, B.N. Maritime-port clusters: an initial diagnosis of the oil and gas *cluster* in the Santos micro-region. eGesta, v. 4, n. 2, p. 35-77, 2008.

MARCOVITCH, J. To change the future: climate change, public policies and business strategies. Sâo Paulo: Editora da Universidade de Sâo Paulo: Saraiva, 2006.

MORAES, A.B.G.; MARTINS, J.V.B. How does understanding demand support innovation in industrial companies? Revista Gestâo Industrial, v. 02, n. 02: p. 34-53, 2006.

ORGANIZATION FOR ECONOMIC COOPERATION AND DEVELOPMENT IN EUROPE - OECD. Oslo Manual. Proposed Guidelines for the Collection and Interpretation of Data on Technological Innovation. 2ª. edition. Translation: FINEP. Brasilia: Ministry of Science and Technology, 2004.

PERUSSI FILHO, S. Strategy creation process in small technology-based companies: proposal for a model covering the phases of development of companies in the medical and dental equipment manufacturing sector. 2006, 166p. Thesis (Doctorate in

Production) - Sâo Carlos School of Engineering, University of Sâo Paulo. São Paulo, 2006.

PORTER, M.E.; KRAMER, M. R. Strategy and society: the link between competitive advantage and corporate social responsibility. Harvard Business Review, v. 84, n. 12, p. 78-92, 2006.

PORTER, M.E. Competitive strategy: techniques for analyzing competition. 17 ed. Rio de Janeiro: Elsevier, 1999a.

PORTER, M. E. Competition On Competition. Essential Competitive Strategies. Rio de Janeiro: Editora. Campus, 1999b.

PEREIRA, M.F.; GRAPEGGIA, M.; EMMENDOERFER, M.L.; TRÊS, D.L. Innovation factors for the survival of micro and small enterprises in Brazil. Revista de Administraçâo e Inovaçâo, v. 6, n. 1, p. 50-65, 2009.

REF, R.; LEE, D. Accenture change management for high-tech companies. 2009. Accenture [on line]. Available at: <http://www.accenture.com/SiteCollectionDocuments/PDF/Accenture-Change-Management-for-High-Tech-Companies.pdf>. Accessed on: June 2, 2013.

SCHUMPETER, J. A. The Theory of Economic Development. Sâo Paulo: Abril, 1982.

SHANE, S. Reflections on the 2010 *AMR* decade award: delivering on the promise of entrepreneurship as a field of research. The Academy of Management Review, Jan, v.37, pp.10-20, 2012.

TIDD, J. Innovation management in context: environment, organization and performance.International Journal of Management Reviews, v. 3, n. 3, p. 169183, 2001.

UNIETHOS. Ethos Institute. Education for social responsibility. 2013. [online]. Available at: <http://www.uniethos.org.br/DesktopDefault.aspx?TabID=3993&Alias=Uniethos&Lang=EN>. Accessed on April 26, 2013.

FEDERAL UNIVERSITY OF LAVRAS. Manual for accessing technology-based ventures to Inbatec's incubation program. Lavras: Federal University of Lavras, 2011.

VAN DER MEER, H. Open Innovation - The Dutch Treat: Challenges in Thinking in Business Models. The Author Journal Compilation, v.16, n.2, 2007.

WONG, P.K.; SINGH, A. The pattern of innovation in the knowledge intensive business services sector of Singapore", Singapore Management Review, v.6, n.1, p. 21-44, 2004.

3 ARTICLE 2: SANTA MARIA'S REGIONAL AND DOMESTIC MARKET: A PROSPECTIVE STUDY OF HIGH-TECH NEEDS

Bàrbara Potter Pereira[1] Janis Elisa Ruppenthal[2]

SUMMARY

Initiatives to create technology parks have been growing in Brazil. However, there needs to be an innovative means of making the establishment of an innovative space effective in the long term, bearing in mind that in order to build an innovative society there needs to be a place with innovative characteristics. Considering that the applied research and development needed to create technological innovation and competitiveness must originate from the companies' perceptions, this paper discusses the profile of the need for innovation development as perceived by the industries of the Corede of the Central Region of Rio Grande do Sul, and is important insofar as it allows companies that may set up in the Santa Maria Technology Park to identify relevant variables that are related to the innovation needs of regional industries. The study enabled the authors to observe that regional industries are open to innovative solutions for their businesses, and that they especially value innovations in the area of processes, products and management technologies. It also indicates that the biggest obstacles to innovation for the companies studied are the high cost of equipment and the lack of qualified personnel, indicating that the creation of innovations related to these problems can constitute business opportunities.

Keywords: Technology-based companies. Innovation. Regional needs .

INTRODUCTION

A new economic order was created as a result of the opening up of markets, and this order was based mainly on the structuring of new forms of production

1 Administrator, Master in Production Engineering from USFM.
2 PhD in Engineering. Professor in the Postgraduate Program at UFSM.

organization, emphasizing competitiveness and technological innovation. Industrial organization quickly began to incorporate innovative ways of producing and facing up to the constant challenges of the market (TALAMO; CARVALHO, 2004).

Innovation is increasingly related to the ability of organizations to remain sustainable, in response to market pressures associated with competitiveness and demand. Companies are forced to adopt strategies to achieve economic efficiency and satisfy their customers' needs, developing value-added products, services, processes and businesses, which also meet the demands of social and environmental responsibility (PORTER, 1999; BARBIERI *et al.*, 2010).

In this way, innovation has become a necessity, and understanding and managing innovation are managerial skills (LOPES; AZEVEDO, 2010).

The new technological paradigm has stimulated changes in the economic, social, cultural, political and behavioral configurations of societies, and in view of this, locations that have favorable conditions for the establishment of industries or segments of industries associated with innovation have been striving to stimulate the creation and/or establishment of networks of innovative organizations (BARQUETTE. 2002; GODOY, 2009).

In this scenario, initiatives to create technology parks have been growing in Brazil. However, it is necessary to have an innovative environment to make the establishment of an innovative space effective in the long term, since in order to build an innovative society it is essential to have a place with innovative characteristics (BARQUETTE. 2002).

Bearing in mind that the applied research and development needed to create technological innovation and competitiveness must originate from companies' perceptions (STEINER *et al.*, 2008), it can be seen that it is organizations, whatever their nature, that must demonstrate what their needs are, their weaknesses, their difficulties to be overcome so that, in this way, their partners can develop solutions that contribute to the development of their competitive capacity and sustainability (BARQUETTE. 2002; STEINER *et al.*, 2008).

In view of these propositions, the research problem that this investigation seeks to elucidate is: what is the profile of regional innovation needs that could constitute opportunities for basic technology companies installed in the Santa Maria Technology Park?

In view of this problem, the general aim of the research is to investigate the main perceptions of the region's industries regarding the development and supply of innovative solutions for them.

This work is important insofar as it allows companies that may set up in the Santa Maria Technology Park to identify relevant variables that are related to the innovation needs of regional industries and to their own sustainability.

TECHNOLOGY-BASED COMPANIES

Technology-based companies, or high-tech companies, are those involved in the design, development and introduction of new products and/or innovative manufacturing processes, through the systematic application of scientific and technological knowledge (BRAD, 2009).

Over the last two decades, companies of this nature have played an important role in the social and economic development of several countries, including the least developed, given their contribution to increasing the number of innovations in products and services with great economic potential; to stimulating progress in science and technology, to motivating entrepreneurship and to their ability to generate new skills (ANDRADE JUNIOR, 2011).

Organizations focused on technology development generate very positive effects on local development, since they generate high economic value, produce innovative goods with high added value, and meet the demands of specific and differentiated clients (ARAÙJO *et al.*, 2005; MINARDI *et al.*, 2013). In addition, they stimulate investment in research and the creation of technologies, and boost the local economy (ARAÙJO *et al.,* 2005),

These companies are relevant as promoters of social development, both because they are creators of innovations and solutions, and because they contribute to tax collection at national and local level, and employ highly qualified people (MACHADO *et al.,* 2005; MINARDI *et al.,* 2013).

Scientific research and the application of knowledge generated by research are the very nature of technology-based companies. Although it is characteristic of them to seek out new markets, adapting technologies for new products, and even going international, because of exports, these companies also operate in small, specific markets, focusing on the strategy of product positioning in niche markets (BERTÉ, 2006).

These organizations are characterized by promoting economic renewal in regions whose traditional sectors of the economy have weakened or become obsolete. Through innovative solutions or products, they create alternatives to redirect their clients' strategy towards the standards prevailing in the competitive landscape. In this sense, by overcoming traditional structures, they drive national development (ANDRADE JUNIOR, 2011).

However, like any business, these types of companies also face challenges and difficulties. These include technical difficulties, the lack of entrepreneurial experience of their managers, difficulties in articulating innovative projects, and obstacles to market penetration (BIZZOTTO *et al.*, 2002).

These companies are also hampered by the fact that decision-making processes are constantly entrusted to technical staff, who don't always have managerial training. Another obstacle is the scarcity of capital to meet the demand for investment needed to create innovative products. This is because traditional investors are reluctant to invest in companies with risky technologies, in markets that are still little known (NETTO, 2006).

The existence of an already traditional tendency to locate research and development activities in large centers or privileged locations, characterized by favourable conditions, can become a challenge when trying to stimulate the spatial dispersion of technological research. This is because the places where research centers are currently located have a long history and circumstances that justify their evolution as research sites (BARQUETTE, 2002).

High-tech companies interested in overcoming the difficulties common to them should seek to link up with other institutions, such as universities and entities that promote and support the development of this type of organization. In addition, they need to analyze their market positioning strategy, improve their network of contacts and elements related to business management (BIZZOTTO *et al.*, 2002).

In this sense, it should be noted that there has been a growing number of initiatives to create technology parks and incubators, which seek to reproduce the ideal conditions for the development of high-tech companies and competitive capacity, similar to what happens in the now mature Silicon Valley in the United States (BARQUETTE, 2002).

In these cases, these companies have the opportunity to develop surrounded by and interrelated with high-level private organizations, educational institutions strongly oriented towards research, and governmental and private research centers, technology parks, as well as other institutions that hold highly aggregating competencies and resources for the developing organizations (BARQUETTE, 2002; STEINER *et al.*, 2008).

TECHNOLOGY PRODUCTION IN TECHNOLOGY PARKS

Technology parks are private ventures in the public interest that aim to transform knowledge into wealth, generating new products and processes. They can be defined as innovation environments, which are typically located close to universities and research centers, due to the beneficial synergies and opportunities established between the institutions (STEINER *et al.*, 2008).

Science and technology parks are important policy instruments for supporting innovation. They also make it possible to transfer technology, generate new jobs and foster economic and social development. They are characterized by providing physical infrastructure that is favourable to the establishment of technology-based companies, which benefit from the agglomeration of companies of the same nature (MACHADO *et al.,* 2005; GARGIONE *et al.*, 2006).

Markman *et al* (2005) state that the growth in the number of technology-based companies setting up in technology parks is explained by the way in which technology is transferred from laboratories to companies, relying on the work of intermediary agents who promote the transfer of technology produced in universities. According to these authors, the interaction between universities and companies generates mutual benefits, and the transfer of technology is an important stimulus to innovation.

Technology parks have a specialized workforce, laboratories and waste treatment infrastructure, as well as other peculiarities designed to maintain an environment for the creation of cutting-edge technology. They are located close to large cities and research centers, not least because they need to have technological capabilities and remain integrated with the market (MACHADO *et al.,* 2005).

METHODOLOGY

The study seeks to identify the profile of the need for innovation development as perceived by Santa Maria's industries. To this end, we want to know the importance of developing innovations for local industries; their willingness to increase investments in research and technology development; the main innovative aspects that these organizations value, and the obstacles that these industries perceive in relation to innovative activities.

This calls for research which, carried out with companies, allows them to know their positions on these aspects. Research, according to Demo (1996), is an everyday activity that translates into a question that is dealt with systematically and critically, allowing us to intervene in reality or promote a critical dialogue that considers all of its theoretical and practical aspects.

The research is of an applied nature, defined by Silva and Meneses (2005) as that which aims to produce knowledge specifically aimed at solving predetermined problems. In the case of this research, it is applied because its findings are immediately applicable to technology-based companies wishing to set up in the Santa Maria Technology Park.

The data collection technique was the structured questionnaire. This type of questionnaire is one in which individuals choose the answer that best represents their opinion through closed questions (GIL, 1999). The questionnaire was submitted to executives from selected industries in the Corede Central region by the researcher herself.

The sample consisted of 14 (fourteen) industries with more than 100 employees, which are part of the region of the Regional Development Council of the Santa Maria region, Corede Central. These industries are located in Santa Maria, Agudo, Itaara, Júlio de Castilhos, Nova Palma and Tupanciretâ. Data was collected in August 2013 and organized using Microsoft *Excel for Windows* software.

The data treatment approach was quantitative. This type of approach translates opinions and information into numbers in order to enable classifications and analysis (SILVA; MENESES, 2005).

Research subjects: industries in the Corede Central region of RS

Coredes is the abbreviation for the Regional Development Councils of Rio Grande do Sul (ESTADO DO RIO GRANDE DO SUL, 2013), created in 1994 by State Law 10.283/94. Their main objective is to "formulate and implement regional strategies, consolidating them into strategic regional development plans" (ESTADO DO RIO GRANDE DO SUL, 2013).

The state of Rio Grande do Sul is subdivided into 28 Coredes, which group together neighboring municipalities. The industries that are of interest to this study are located in the municipalities that are part of Corede Central, which is based in the municipality of Santa Maria, where the Santa Maria Industrial Park is located.

According to the Industrial Register of the Federation of Industries of Rio Grande do Sul (FIERGS, 2012), the Corede Central region has 28 industries with more than 50 employees, but only 14 of these companies took part in the study, making up a sample of 50% of the total universe.

PROFILE OF THE NEED TO DEVELOP INNOVATIONS

The responses obtained from the executives of the industries investigated constitute the following findings:

The importance of developing innovations

Of the 14 participating companies, 57% say that innovation is *very important* for their organization. Another 43% consider it *important*.

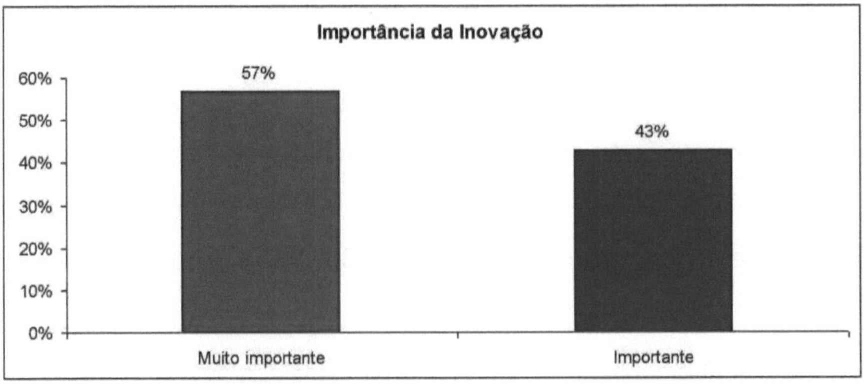

Figure 1 - The importance of developing innovations.

Source: The author

This positioning of organizations in relation to innovations is in line with the propositions that assert innovations as a fundamentally important element, even for the survival of companies in the market (PORTER, 1999; BARBIERI *et al.*, 2010).

In this sense, the industries in the Corede Central region are also aware of the strategic importance of innovation, and this fact in itself is an indicator that the companies in the region could constitute a local consumer market for the technology-based companies that set up in the region. And the existence of a local customer base, as Porter (1999) states, enables companies to create and sustain competitive advantages in specific fields.

Willingness to increase investment in research and technology development

When asked if they intend to increase their investment in research and technology development over the next five years, 13 of the 14 companies surveyed said yes, making up 93%.

This is a relevant fact to be taken into account by basic technology companies wishing to set up in the Santa Maria Technology Park. It implies that they operate in an environment that contributes to improving their ability to sustain themselves and their competitiveness, taking into account that interactions with local clients are opportunities from a technological point of view (PORTER, 1999; BERCOVICH; SWANKE, 2003; PEREIRA and RUPPENTHAL, 2013).

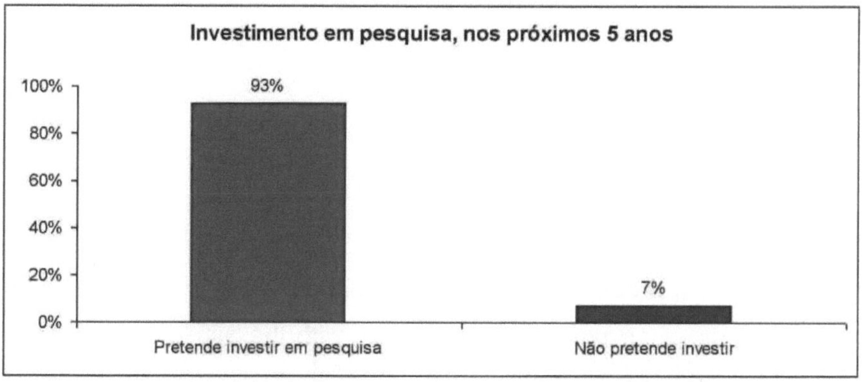

Figure 2 - Investment in research over the next 5 years.

Source: The author

What's more, investment in research and innovation, as some authors point out , reflects the most mature perception of industrial entrepreneurs about the direction of the country's development (VEIGA, 2010; TUOMI and CASTRO NETO, 2013).

Main innovative aspects valued by the organization

With regard to the main innovative aspects valued by the organization, respondents were asked to indicate two of these. Eventually, some people wanted to indicate just one aspect, giving a total score of 27 answers.

Process innovation is the most highly valued by the industries consulted. Product innovation also stands out among the most valued by Corede Central industries, followed by innovations in management technology, equipment development and people training.

These responses are reflected in the percentages seen in the figure below.

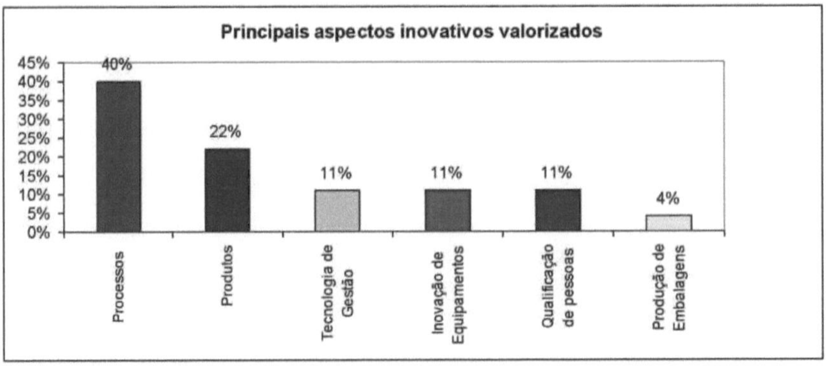

Figure 3 - The aspects that are important for innovation

Source: The author

In order to make new products and processes viable, research is essential, as it enables products to be created or perfected, with the aim of making them better, cheaper and more competitive (DELBEM, 2005). Innovations occupy a central position in technological development and must meet the needs of society and the market. For there to be economic development, there must be demand for new products and new production processes (SCHUMPETER, 1982).

Companies in the Corede Central region see the importance of innovations in processes as well as products. This in itself is strategic information for technology companies setting up in the region. Knowing that there is a business community that is open to innovations and willing to invest in them, and knowing that processes and products are the aspects that most interest companies in the region, makes it easier for prospective companies to build their strategic plans.

Obstacles to innovation

Among the obstacles perceived by the industries surveyed in relation to innovative activities are:

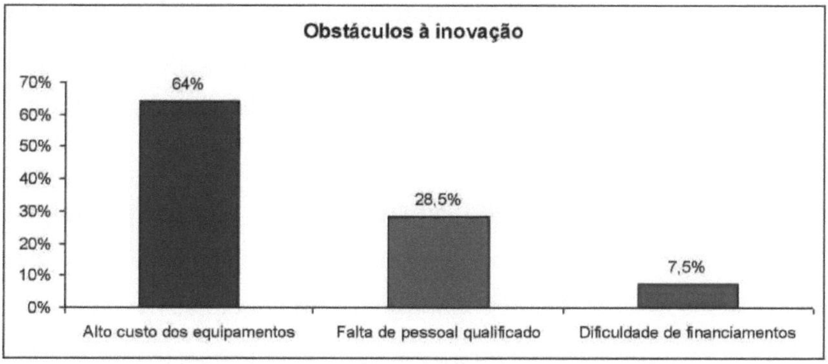

Figure 4 - Obstacles observed in relation to innovative initiatives

Source: The author

The high cost of equipment is the biggest obstacle perceived by local industries in formulating an innovative project. This is followed by the lack of qualified personnel.

In line with this, a survey carried out by the Federation of Industries of the State of São Paulo - FIESP (2007), shows that the high cost of investments in machinery and equipment is one of the biggest obstacles to innovation in that state, demonstrating the need for innovative solutions to this problem.

In turn, the lack of people with the necessary qualifications and the scarcity of external technical services create substantial difficulties for the success of innovations, which must be overcome by the institutions (RIGHETTI , 2007; BERTONI and OLIVEIRA, 2010). In addition, policies are needed to train researchers to meet the market's need for technological innovation (RIGHETTI , 2007).

These data show that innovations capable of minimizing equipment costs, as well as technology for training people, by providing solutions for the region's industries, can constitute business opportunities for basic technology companies in the Corede Central region.

FINAL CONSIDERATIONS

Analysis of the profile of innovation development needs perceived by industry in the region studied reveals that regional industries are open to innovative solutions for their businesses, and therefore constitute an interesting market for inbound technology companies.

In addition, the survey shows that the industries listed in the study intend to invest in research to develop innovative solutions, especially those related to the areas of processes, products and management technologies.

In addition, the research also showed that the biggest obstacles to innovation for companies in the Central Region of Rio Grande do Sul, which are the high cost of equipment and the lack of qualified personnel, are also opportunities for innovation and business for companies that set up in the Santa Maria Technology Park or anywhere in the region.

REFERENCES

ANDRADE JUNIOR, P. P. Reflections on the economic and technological impacts on work organization in technology-based companies. Economia & Tecnologia, v 27, p. 135-142, 2011.

ARAÙJO, M. H.; LAGO, R. M.; OLIVEIRA, L. C. A.; CABRAL, P. R. M.; CHENG, L. C.; BORGES, C.; FILION, L. J. Academic *spin-off*: creating wealth from knowledge and research. Quimica Nova, v. 28, p. s23- s35, 2005.

BARBIERI, J.C.; VASCONCELOS, I.F.G.; ANDREASSI, T.; VASCONCELOS, F.C. Innovation and sustainability: new models and propositions. Revista de Administraçâo - RAE, v. 50 - n. 2 - apr./jun. 2010 - 146-154

BARQUETTE, S. Location factors for incubators and high-tech ventures. - Revista de Administraçâo de Empresas, v. 42, n. 3, p. 101-113, 2002.

BERTÉ, E.C.O. Contributions to the strategy formulation process of small technology-based companies. 2006. 161 p. Thesis

(Doctorate in Administration) - University of Sâo Paulo, Sâo Paulo, 2006.

BERTONI, R.B.; OLIVEIRA, V.C.P. Is the lack of internal capacity within firms an obstacle to innovation in Brazil? Pontifical Catholic University. 2010. [on line]. Available at:

<http://www.pucsp.br/eitt/downloads/21_12_10/xi-ciclo-de-debates/xi-ciclo-rebeca-bertoni-vanessa.pdf>. Accessed on: September 12, 2013.

BIZZOTTO, C.; DALFOVO, O.; SENA, A.; FALLGATTER, M. G. H. Accompanying and guiding incubated companies. In: SEMINARIO DE PARQUE TECNOLÓGICO E INCUBADORA DE EMPRESAS, Sâo Paulo, 2002. Proceedings... Sâo Paulo. SP: ANPROTEC, 2002. v. 1. CD ROM.

BRAD, S. Equating Business Value of Innovative Product Ideas. 19th CIRP Design Conference. Cranfield University, p.526, 2009. [on line]. Available at:

<https://dspace.lib.cranfield.ac.uk/bitstream/1826/3651/3/Equating_Business_Value_of_Innovative_Product_Ideas-2009.pdf>. Accessed on: September

30, 2013

DELBEM, A. B. C. Main aspects related to the development of technological innovation projects through university-company cooperation. In: SIMPÒSIO DE ENGENHARIA DE PRODUÇÂO, 2005, 12. Baurù. Electronic proceedings... Available at: <www.simpep.feb.unesp.br/anais/.../copiar.php?...Principais_aspectos.pdf>. Accessed on: 11 Sep 209.

DEMO, P. Educar pela pesquisa. Campinas, Sâo Paulo: Autores Associados, 1996.

GARGIONE, L.A.; LOURENÇÂO, P.T.M.; PLONSKI, G.A. Critical elements for modeling private technology parks in Brazil. In: SIMPÓSIO DE GESTÂO DA INOVAÇÂO TECNOLÓGICA, Gramado, 2006. Proceedings... Gramado, RS: ANPAD, 2006. [on line]. Available at: <http://www.anpad.org.br/diversos/trabalhos/Simp%C3%B3sio/simposio_2006/IPP/2006_IPP819.pdf>. Accessed on: September 2, 2013.

GIL, A. C. Métodos e Técnicas de Pesquisa Social. 5. ed. Sâo Paulo: Atlas, 1999.

GODOY, R.S. Relationships between organizational culture and innovation processes in technology-based companies. 2009. 212 P. Dissertaçâo (Master's Degree in Production Engineering) - Universidade Federal de Sâo Carlos, Sâo Carlos, 2009.

LOPES, F.; AZEVEDO, S. Execution of the GIT/PR project. In: FAYET, E.A. Managing innovation. A challenge for companies. Curitiba : IEL/PR, 2010.

MACHADO, H.P.V.; CASTRO, S.C.; SILVA, M.A. An approach to technology parks and the creation of technology-based companies. In: ENCONTRO DE ESTUDOS SOBRE EMPREENDEDORISMO E GESTAO DE PEQUENAS EMPRESAS, 4, 2005, Curitiba, Anais... Curitiba, 2005, p.101-110.

MALHoTRA, N. K. Marketing Research: An Applied Orientation. 4. ed. Porto Alegre: Bookman, 2006.

MARKMAN, G.; PHAN, P.; BALKIN, D.B.; GIANoDIS, P. Entrepreneurship and university-based technology transfer. Journal of Business Venturing, v.20, p.241-263, 2005.

MINARDI, B.E.C.; VITA, F.L.; SoUZA, F.S.L.; FARIA, A.F. Model for the study of *spin-offs* from a technology-based business incubator. Revista Eletrônica Produçâo & Engenharia, v. 4, n. 1, p. 374-384, 2013.

NETTo, A.V. Gestâo de pequenas e médias empresas de base tecnológica. Barueri, SP: Minha Editora; Brasilia, DF: SEBRAE, 2006.

PEREIRA, B.P.; RUPPENTHAL, J.E. The importance of the local market in the sustainability of new technology-based ventures: a study from Porter's perspective. Espacios, v.34, n.6, p.16, 2013.

PORTER, M.E. Competitive strategy: techniques for analyzing competition. 17 ed. Rio de Janeiro: Elsevier, 1999.

RIGHETTI, S. The effectiveness of an innovation system depends on highly qualified professionals. Inovaçâo Uniemp, v.3 n.5, p.32-37, 2007.

STEINER, J.E.; CASSIM, M.B.; RoBAZZI, A.C. Technology Parks: Innovation Environments. 2008. University of São Paulo. [on line]. Available at:

<http://www.iea.usp.br/publicacoes/textos/steinercassimrobazziparquestec.pdf>. Accessed on: Aug. 26, 2013.

SILVA, E L. ; MENESES, E. M. Metodologia da Pesquisa e Elaboração de Dissertaçâo. 3ª ed. Florianópolis: UFSC, 2005.

TALAMO, J.R.; CARVALHO, M.M. Selection of the fundamental objectives of a business cooperation network. Gestâo & Produçâo, v.11, n.2, p.239250, 2004.

TUOMI, K.; CASTRO NETO, L. Innovation and Venture Capital Policy in Brazil and South Africa. Journal of Technology Management & Innovation, v.8, n.2, p. 35-46, 2013.

VEIGA, J.E.Economia politica da qualidade. Rev. adm. Empres, v.50, n.3, p. 338-344, 2010.

4 DISCUSSION

Several countries have sought to reproduce the conditions necessary for the creation and development of technology-based companies ((BARQUETTE, 2002, PALETTA, 2008), since these companies have the characteristic of being intensive creators of innovations (SANTOS, 2004; ANDRADE JUNIOR, 2012), which are essential for competitiveness between companies and between nations (PORTER, 1999; GARGIONE *et al.*, 2006).

In the same vein, the installation of a technology park in Santa Maria should provide the region with companies whose nature is characterized by the creation of innovations, which will enable them to meet the needs of internal and external innovation solutions in the city and the region.

Entrepreneurs in a given market are dependent on the relationships they establish at their local level, and the decisive characteristics of a location enable their companies to create and sustain competitive advantages, provided there is a healthy relationship between the social and economic players (PORTER, 1999; BARQUETTE, 2002).

High-tech production is important and beneficial for productive environments, since innovation is essential for competitiveness and can generate quality and cost advantages, which translate into benefits for companies and their customers. But the success of innovation requires a local market that influences its ability to sustain itself and its competitiveness.

For the industries in the Corede Central region involved in this research, innovation is seen as *very important* or *important*, demonstrating that companies in the region are aware of the competitive importance of innovations, as pointed out by various authors (PORTER, 1999a; CASAROTTO FILHO, 2001; BARROS *et al.*, 2010; BARBIERI et *al.*, 2010).

Investments in research are of great importance for the development of innovations and technologies with a high potential to generate profit in the market (FONSECA *et al.*, 2012), and the fact that around 93% of the companies surveyed declared their willingness to increase their investments over the next five years is a strong indication that interactions with regional clients constitute business opportunities for companies developing technologies and innovations (PORTER, 1999; BERCOVICH; SWANKE, 2003; PEREIRA and RUPPENTHAL, 2013).

This means that the market in which companies that produce high technology operate must be characterized by an environment conducive to the production of innovation, which will affect their performance and opportunities (PORTER, 1999; BARQUETTE, 2002).

Such an environment must include variables such as highly qualified personnel; closer relations with local companies, and feedback of information that will serve as a subsidy to the companies that produce technologies, indicating whether or not they are closer to meeting the needs of their customers. It is important to note that the spatial proximity of related and supporting sectors, upstream and downstream, facilitates the exchange of information and ideas that lead to innovation (PORTER, 1998; JOÂO, 2008).

It is important for companies to interact with demanding consumers as a way of preparing themselves to face the competitive demands that shape today's globalized markets (PORTER, 1999; BARROS *et al.*, 2010).

These consumers have their needs, which must be understood and met, as they are critical factors in creating new market opportunities (MORAES and MARTINS, 2006; EDLER and GEORGHIOU, 2007).

It is organizations of all kinds that must demonstrate their needs, critical points and difficulties to be overcome, so that their partners can develop solutions favorable to the development of their ability to compete and sustain themselves (BARQUETTE. 2002; STEINER *et al.*, 2008).

In turn, science and technology parks have functioned as innovation support centers, enabling the transfer of technology as well as the economic and social development of localities and/or regions (MACHADO *et al.,* 2005; GARGIONE *et al.*, 2006). The

organizations that are part of it need to have technological capabilities and to remain integrated with the market (MACHADO *et al.,* 2005).

Technology-based companies that are part of technology parks are organizations that specialize in developing technologies and innovations in products, processes or services resulting from applied research (BRASIL, 2000; PERUSSI FILHO, 2006; UNIVERSIDADE FEDERAL DE LAVRAS, 2011). These are precisely the main innovative aspects valued by the industries of Corede Central.

One thing that needs to be taken into account is that industries sometimes want to innovate, but encounter difficulties of various kinds. In the case of the Corede Central region, the difficulties in innovating are related to the cost of equipment. This is in line with information from FIESP (2007), which points out that São Paulo industries have the same concern.

It should be noted, however, that the perception of difficulties can be an opportunity for companies that are attentive to their customers' needs (SCHUMPETER, 1984; STEPHENS and PARTRIDGE, 2011).

5 CONCLUSION

This work made it possible to identify how the dynamics of the local and regional market in Santa Maria can influence the performance of technology-based companies set up in the Santa Maria Technology Park.

Initially, it should be noted that innovation is essential to competitiveness and can generate quality and cost advantages, which translate into benefits for companies and their customers.

Analysis of the theoretical framework also allows us to see that entrepreneurs in a given market are dependent on the relationships they establish at their local level and, at the same time as they are able to influence this market, they are also influenced by it. Furthermore, certain aspects are particularly decisive in these relationships.

With regard to the elements of Corede Central that can influence the ability of technology-based ventures to sustain themselves and their competitiveness, it was observed that the ability of technology-based ventures to sustain themselves and their competitiveness can be influenced by the availability of highly qualified personnel, by the existence of a close relationship between the companies that develop technologies and local/regional industries, and also by the opportunities for product experimentation, evaluations and *feedback*, which make it possible to improve the quality of production.

In addition, the dynamics of the local and regional market can contribute positively to improving the performance of technology-based companies if there are demanding customers among the industries in the region, who will be able to motivate these industries to promote continuous improvement in the quality of their innovative products/services.

With regard to the profile of the regional innovation needs of the industries in the Corede Central region, it was found that the region's industries are open to offering innovative solutions for their businesses, and that products, processes and management technologies are the focus of their innovation interests.

As for the aspects that hinder innovation, in the perception of the industries of Corede Central, their representatives point out that the cost of equipment, as well as the lack of qualified personnel, are their biggest obstacles when it comes to innovative practices.

As a suggestion for a follow-up to this study, there is a need for studies to be carried out with the technology-based companies participating in the Santa Maria Technology Park, to assess whether they have developed studies on the needs of regional industries, and if so, whether their results corroborate the data found in this investigation.

In addition, it may be worth investigating whether the obstacles that regional organizations associate with innovation constitute research and development opportunities for incoming technology-based companies.

REFERENCES

ANDRADE JUNIOR, P.P. Cluster analysis of performance factors of technology-based companies in incubators: a study of incubators in the State of Santa Catarina. Revista Produçâo Online, Florianópolis, SC, v.12, n. 1, p. 205-228, 2012. Available at: <http://www.producaoonline.org.br/rpo/article/view/868>. Accessed on: September 14, 2013.

ARAGAO, I.M. Post-incubation of technology-based companies. 2005. 101 p. Thesis (Doctorate in Administration) - University of Sâo Paulo, Sâo Paulo, 2005.

STATE OF RIO GRANDE DO SUL. Popular consultation. Coredes - Regional Development Councils of Rio Grande do Sul. 2013. Available at: <http://www.consultapopular.rs.gov.br/conteudo_puro.asp?ta=1&modo_exibi c ao=&cod_menu=31>. Accessed on: September 15, 2013.

FEDERATION OF INDUSTRIES OF THE STATE OF RIO GRANDE DO SUL. - FIERGS. Industrial Register of Rio Grande do Sul 2013, 2013. CD-ROM.

FEDERATION OF INDUSTRIES OF THE STATE OF SAO PAULO. FIESP survey. Innovation needs in São Paulo industry. Sâo Paulo: FIESP System, 2007.

GARGIONE, L.A. A model for financing technology parks in Brazil. Exploring the potential of investment funds. 2011. 345 p. Thesis (Doctorate in Engineering) - University of Sâo Paulo, Sâo Paulo, 2011.

PALETTA, F.C. Information technology, innovation and entrepreneurship: critical success factors in the use of management tools in incubated technology-based companies. 2008. 156 p. Thesis (Doctorate in Sciences) - University of Sâo Paulo, Sâo Paulo, 2008.

PORTER, M.E. Competitive strategy: techniques for the analysis and competition. 17 ed. Rio de Janeiro: Elsevier, 1999.

SANTOS, S.A.; ALMEIDA, F.R.; TAKAHASHI, A.R.W. Comparing the barriers and facilities for the creation and development of new technology-based companies (NTBFS) in Brazil and abroad. In: SIMPÒSIO DE GESTAO DA INOVAÇÂO TECNOLÓGICA, 23., October 19-22, 2004, Curitiba. Electronic proceedings... Sâo Paulo, Available at: <http://www.ead.fea.usp.br/eadonline/grupodepesquisa/publica%C3%A7%C3%B5es/francisco/6.pdf>. Accessed on September 14, 2013.

SILVA, E. L.; MENESES, E.M. Metodologia da Pesquisa e Elaboração de Dissertaçâo. Florianópolis: UFSC, 2005.

STEPHENS, H.M.; PARTRIDGE, M. Do Entrepreneurs Enhance Economic Growth in Lagging Regions? Growth and Change, v.42, n.4, p.431-465, 2011.

MIX
Papier aus verantwortungsvollen Quellen
Paper from responsible sources
FSC® C105338

Printed by Books on Demand GmbH, Norderstedt / Germany